# Beauty From *Ashes*

## Helping A Generation Recover From Childhood Sexual Molestation And Abuse!

# INGRIT M. BUSBEE

This book is dedicated to YOU, to US!
The ones who survived the theft of our
innocence, learning to be strong before we
even felt safe. Finding beauty in the
ashes of our pain.

# Acknowledgements

First and foremost, I acknowledge and give all honor, praise, and anything else I can give to my Lord and Savior Jesus Christ! Without Him, I am truly nothing, and with Him, I am everything that I choose to be! He is truly my Father!

To my husband, my man of God, the one I want to talk to at the start and end of every day, the one who has carried me when I couldn't carry myself! Thank you for being you!

To my children, you are the very essence of God's manifested love in my life.

To my family, I am so blessed to be your blood.

To Pastors Creflo and Taffi Dollar; to my spiritual parents Michael and Connie Smith; and to my Pastors Danny and Jamie Schulz, I am not the woman of grace that I am, without the people of grace that you are. Thank you all for never giving up on us.

To my friends, too many to name. Oh, how blessed I am. Thank YOU! Each and every one!

And to readers and supporters of this book, please know that wherever you are right now is only a small part of your story. Keep going to sleep and waking up, the world needs you. You are loved!

# Contents

# Chapter 1
# THE INTRO!

*"For I know the plans I have for you,
says The Lord, plans for good
and to give you an expected end!"*
*Jeremiah 29:11 (NLT)*

First and foremost, let me explicitly express that I'm not a doctor, nor am I certified as a therapist or any type of licensed counselor. I'm writing this book only by the wisdom of the Holy Spirit and my own life experiences.

With that being said, I would probably have never thought to write this if I didn't believe that God himself hadn't told me too!

I'm in my bathroom, not very long ago, and I heard the voice of God as clear as I ever had, saying to me, "Write THIS book..."

## BEAUTY FROM ASHES
## Helping A Generation Recover From Childhood Molestation And Sexual Abuse!

I immediately went to my husband and cried in his arms because I knew what that meant. It meant tapping into a world that I had long left behind and waking up demons that I was absolutely good with letting sleep.

But with his encouragement and my heart committed to God, I accepted the task and prayed that I can do justice to what Daddy God was expecting of me.

So, let's go on a journey. From the years of eight to ten-years-old, I was sexually molested by a grown man! Full blown sex. It's crazy what can be remembered when it needs to be and what can also be suppressed for the same reason. I wanted to make it clear that it was a grown man.

I understand that this isn't everyone's experience. Some were molested by grown men like me, some by grown women, and others were molested by other kids very similar to themselves.

Regardless of who or what, molestation is a robber! The act itself is the ability to take advantage of!

I'm writing this as a part of Generation X, but in all reality, this has been going on since the beginning of time, generation after generation. As far back as any history can be read, there is the story of a child being inappropriately introduced to sex.

What's really crazy, is as I started writing this book, I actually was able to remember the very moment that the molestation actually began. Not the physical touch, or the day he stated, "Let's play a game," but the actual day. He opened the bathroom door when I was sitting in the bathtub and stared at me for far too long.

I think back on that moment, now as an adult and wonder, why didn't something click in his mind and tell him, don't do that? Don't look at her like that. She's a baby. She's a child! But I assume now that the demons that had long haunted him before he met me were only definitely familiar enough with me not to tell him that!

What does that mean? I believe in the power of the spiritual realm, and I believe that many times, demonic forces are assigned to your life. Their mission is to abort any assignment that has been given to you before your life even began. Those forces are able to tap into your future resistance of the demonic kingdom and also see the weight and the monumental understanding of authority that you will have in the Kingdom of God. Therefore, just like he did with Jesus, the enemy puts out a search team to attempt your demise! But we will talk more about that later.

A few years ago, God gave me this word. He said,

## "Knowing who you are
## is vital!"

I wish I could say I knew exactly what that meant when it was spoken to me, but my understanding is so clear now.

Why is it that the attack of identity always occurs when we're young? The molestation happened when you were a child. The bullying, the rape or sexual assault occurred during your teen years or early college years. Your dad left, your mom left, the drug addiction occurred when you were young. Because the enemy is smart. If he can attack us when we're most vulnerable, then we carry that false identity throughout our life. We walk around as adults, even after salvation, not knowing who we really are.

To me, when I thought about it, we must be a really big threat to the devil for him to try to destroy us at such a young age.

I wasn't sure what that passage from God meant when I wrote it more than three years ago, but I certainly know what it means now. To know yourself is to know who you are and whose you are! It's your protection! As you get to the end of this story—because that's what it is... a story, my story—I know that you will understand what it means also!

The purpose of this book is to lead you, the reader, to heal. My heart has grieved for many years watching my generation, specifically women, not be healed from their childhood trauma of molestation.

It's always so obvious when I see it! I'm truly never shocked when I'm in conversation with someone and they tell me that they've been molested or even when I'm watching the brokenness of celebrities or people of the world show the obvious fruit of having their innocence stolen.

Healing is a process. And I'm talking about total healing! I'm talking about healing with no residue of that past pain at all. That's the healing that God wants all of us to have! That's the healing that He sent His son to the cross for. That is the healing that is available if you trust and believe and put in the work!

What is the work, you ask?

The work is actually resting! How do you rest and work at the same time? First, by getting to know Christ intimately. Second, by working to study, and speaking and believing in His finished works. Then resting in the knowing that those finished works will force you into the healing that is rightfully yours!

My Spiritual Dad, Michael T. Smith, once taught that some of the most traumatic wounds we received in our life can be compared to the scarring of an oak tree. You can take a knife and create a huge scar in an oak tree while it's still a sapling and even though that tree will still continue to grow big and strong and stand for hundreds of years, you can still find that scar exactly where the knife made it.

In many cases, this is what happens to us when we have been inappropriately introduced to sex! It's like an internal scarring or bruising that never goes away, and for most of us, never gets healed.

Before we go any further, let's bring clarity to some things. At this time, you may or may not agree with me, but that's okay. You purchased this book, or it was given to you by someone who knew it would benefit you. Even though you still have your doubts, treat it like an early morning gym workout: you definitely will not want to do it immediately, but by the end, you're happy you did!

So, the first understanding I want you to have is that sex is not bad! Sex was created by God. However, as with anything that God creates, sex has a purpose. It was and is a gift to the married couple, and also an avenue for the married couple to procreate. "Bring forth" is the way its Latin root is described; to reproduce children. In many cases, when people—men and women—have been traumatized sexually, they only understand sex for the procreate part. They totally never get that sex was supposed to be a beautiful and exciting experience for them.

Many (though not all) sexual addicts and or sexual dysfunction, usually stem from sexual trauma as well. For a long time, I worked in an HIV clinic, and I can't tell you the number of clients I had who described to me some type of horrific trauma from their childhood. Most of them involve sexual trauma.

This is such a shared pain and it's far time that we stop being the generation who continues to walk around as if we're okay when we're not. There is a healing waiting for us, specific to us, and for some reason, I have been chosen to help lead you to it!

You no longer have to make fear-based choices for your life. You no longer have to overprotect your children out of fear that what happened to you will happen to them. You no longer have to sleep with anyone other than your spouse to fulfill an inappropriate need to feel temporarily wanted or needed.

**You can be whole,
you can be strong,
and you can be healed!**

# Chapter 2
# STRONGHOLDS!

*"For we do not wrestle against flesh and blood,*
*but against the rulers, against the authorities,*
*against the cosmic powers over the present*
*darkness, against the spiritual forces of evil*
*in the heavenly places."*
*Ephesians 6:12 (ESV)*

Memories can be very difficult at times. The reason why they are, is most times we aren't even trying to remember when all of a sudden, based on a particular circumstance, your mind can go back to something that you have tried to forget.

That happens a lot after sexual abuse, particularly when you are trying to be in a healthy sexual relationship!

A huge part of healing is learning how to be in control of what pictures pop in your head. Most times, many of our reactions stem from something that has resurfaced in our soul (our thinker, feeler, and chooser) and our response to a situation isn't really who we are or how we want to respond but just a reaction to a stronghold!

What is a stronghold you ask? A stronghold can be defined as a "habitual pattern of thought!" It's usually when some type of trauma has occurred in your life and your mind wants to keep replaying it like a movie. Like constantly hitting the rewind button in a movie that you actually despise!

This is the number one strategy of the enemy, the dark one, the evil one. He wants our mind to stay parked at whatever bad thing that has happened to us in the past or whatever bad things that we have caused to happen! When episodes such as these occur in our mind, they are the very definition of "strongholds!"

The issue with strongholds is their ability to lock you into a thought and hold you hostage by creating an emotional response that is probably not indicative of your current life state. Everything in life could be going well, but a painful, past memory will pop into your mind and depending on how long you allow it to stay there, will determine how dark of a space you create.

That's the strength which defines "strong," and the length of time defines the "hold" part. And now you are spiraling in sadness, anxiety, depression or any of several negative emotions for much longer than you desired.

We have to gain control by using our words to deliver us out! You can't sit there and battle a thought with a thought; you must use your words! Your words are a powerful force given to you by God to create and design the very life that you desire. When you speak something, it's very important that you understand that you may have just spoken or given life to an actual thing. Words actually have the ability to harm or heal as well as change the very thought pattern that may be trying to derail your life.

If you are in a car and want to go anywhere, the first thing you have to do is get out of park and put the gear in drive! Without switching gears, you will stay parked and never get to a different or better place!

This is what happens to so many of us after molestation or sexual abuse! We find ourselves stuck in a pattern—whether it's a pattern of unforgiveness, a pattern of addiction, or a pattern of bad choices!

That pattern can also be a pattern that may not seem as 'bad,' per se, like a pattern of overworking, overspending or overeating! It doesn't matter, you're parked, and you need to switch gears!

Once you discover that you've been in this space for far too long, especially a space that causes continual damage to you mentally and or physically, you must speak to it, and remind it:

> ## "I am no longer going to let this (fill in the blank) rob me of a good day!"

When you have not been healed from sexual abuse, you will continue to make bad choices that actually seem to have nothing to do with your abuse, but in reality, is the sum total and reason why you do what you do!

So many of the problems that we encounter in our adult life are usually the direct result of the molestation and trauma we encountered as kids: the consistent bad relationships, the promiscuity, the mismanagement of money, the unstableness, the distrust of people... just to name a few! As much as we try to live a normal life, we just can't seem to tap into it.

Oh, but the answer is here! It's been here all the time! The answer is Jesus! "Jesus is the answer" is not just a cute saying or cliché. He is really the answer to get you to the place of wholeness that your heart desires to be, but your mind and actions keep forfeiting. Not the religious, superhero Jesus we see in movies and pictures, nor the one people sometimes claim to know but you never see any inward or outward change in them at all, but the true Jesus that lives on the inside of you and wants to lead and guide you to the life that you deserve.

Although this chapter is about strongholds, it's really about how to rid yourself of them! The "habitual patterns of thinking" won't matter at all if you don't know how to fix it.

Since we're talking about healing from molestation, and childhood sexual abuse, let's use some of those possible thoughts as examples and the best person that I can use is myself!

A traumatic thought that I had to deal with most of my life because of molestation was the thought that sex was love! For most of my young teen and adult life, I believed that if someone had sex with me, then they loved me.

Well, how silly is that, you say.

It wasn't silly at all to me, because that's how sex was introduced to me: a person that I felt loved me and, in my mind being a child, had sex with me, so I felt like this is what people who loved you do to you.

I carried that thought pattern (habitual thought pattern) into my adult life, UNTIL I gained the true knowledge of Christ! Not church, but a true relationship with Christ! The Anointed one, the One who is the full embodiment of God's love and His grace.

Yes, it starts with the Bible, but your relationship with Christ has to become so intimate and real to the point where you have to know Him as if there is no Bible! When you know Him at that point, He will lead you and help you to think soberly. He will help to guide your thoughts!

Jesus himself helped me to understand the preciousness of my body and that those thoughts were unhealthy, causing me a lot of pain in my life. But His love was so beautiful and able to erase all of the pain and turn it all around as if those thoughts were never mine!

Having almost completed my book, I realized that I should not take lightly the introduction of Christ to you! I've mentioned Him several times and I really want to make sure you understand how vital His presence in your life is. He is the only true definition of love and grace and should always have a proper introduction!

You: Hi, (fill in your name) so glad to meet you!

My name is Ingrit, and I want to introduce you to Jesus The Christ! The anointed one, the all-knowing, all-powerful, all giving and all loving one! He already knows you but sometimes our knowledge of Him is so limited, skewed, and distorted, that it takes someone like me to reintroduce you to what you are missing!

First and foremost, there is no love greater than that of the love that He has for you, and on top of that there is nothing you can do to change His mind about loving you!

He's a healer of your past, and the enhancer of your future! His only goal is to see you win! He's always there for you, and no matter how bad or great things may get in life, He will always be there for you!

I'm sure you have heard other things, but I'm here as a living witness, to tell you that Jesus is the greatest gift we could ever receive! Don't discard what He wants to do in your life!

# Chapter 3
# FORGIVING IS OVERRATED!

*"Bear with each other and forgive one another,*
*if any of you has a grievance against someone.*
*FORGIVE AS THE LORD FORGAVE YOU!"*
Colossians 3:13 (NIV)

Forgiving is so overrated!!

I say that with the most humble heart! People walk around outside of your circumstance telling you to forgive like it's just as easy as deciding on a restaurant to eat at! Many people have been through some very grievous situations and forgiving the one who caused that pain can absolutely not seem possible!

But I'm here to tell you that it is possible and is needed in this process of healing.

How is it possible? you might add.

Well, definitely not the way most of us were taught!

Actually, that's the issue, for most of us, we were not taught how to forgive at all! We were told to forgive and that's what can seem impossible.

In this section of the journey, I want to help teach you how to forgive! Trust me, I understand if you feel like you may not want to forgive! I can absolutely relate because I was once at that place too. Additionally, I got that same sermon from many good-hearted people throwing the verse Matthew 6:14-15 out at me:

> *But If you do not forgive others, your Heavenly Father will not forgive your offenses. (CSB)*

So, really, God, I'm supposed to forgive the adult man who had sex with me when I was a child and didn't even know what sex was?! I am supposed to forgive all of the people who were supposed to protect me and did not?! The ones who only wanted to protect themselves?! I'm supposed to just forgive those who made me feel ashamed for telling my story, as if being molested as a young child was my fault?!

Well, I don't know how to do that; and most importantly, I don't even know if that's even possible!

If I ever had a time in my life when I think I was angry at God, it was when I came across that scripture! Not only was I angry for myself but also the millions of others who had similar stories. Or the mothers who had lost a child to violence, or the fathers who had lost family members because of racist hearts.

I could go on and on with the number of reasons why this scripture didn't make sense, and if it doesn't make sense, then for me, it just wasn't possible.

And so, I went on for a very long time, with a tinge of bitterness because some issues I was able to work out but others not so much.

Forgiveness was not an option until one day when I realized that the bitterness was no longer a tinge but an overwhelming river that flooded my heart and my soul. I didn't know what to do!!

I cried out to God that I not only didn't know how to forgive, but I didn't know if I wanted to!

One of the most important lessons I've learned on this journey is to be honest with God and with myself! Both entities are already aware of the truth, so lying to either of them only delays the inevitable.

As I begin to cry out to Him for answers, He responds in love specific to me as He always has. He heard my cry and simply answered my heart.

The second part of my prayer, which was communicating that I didn't even want to forgive, was answered first. Not wanting to forgive is a part of our human nature! A part of the human experience! Most times we want what we think is justice. We won't always admit it, but we want blood! We want people to suffer and feel the pain that we felt or may still be feeling!

But that's not our true nature. That's not the desire of our spirit man, the part of us that is most like God!

When we become true sons and daughters of God, we are sons and daughters of grace! Grace is our teacher! It is the full embodiment of Christ, which is why it is vital to life that you have your own personal relationship with Him!

As your relationship becomes more intimate with him, day by day, month by month and year by year, grace will be who you are, who you become, and even who you will want to be! We are grace people: we receive grace, and we learn to give grace! This is the key to forgiveness!

We can't discuss forgiveness without talking about "unforgiveness!" Why? you ask. Because this story is to help you get to your healing, and a ginormous part of healing is understanding how and what unforgiveness is and what it does!

I once heard someone say, "Unforgiveness is like you taking a poisonous pill and expecting the other person who hurt you to die!" Imagine that you are literally dying slowly from poison and this person who actually has done this grievous act is walking around, living their best life!

How is that possible? Because you haven't learned the art of forgiveness and are trapped in the cycle of unforgiveness!

Unforgiveness allows whatever the trauma that you experienced to keep occurring. You give the person and the situation power to rule your life!

I call it an art form because that is simply what it is. Art doesn't really have a definition. And the confined cycle of what happens to us internally because of unforgiveness also cannot be defined.

Forgiving someone or even yourself of a grievous act can sometimes seem impossible, but that's only because we have been trying to do it by our own strength.

Our own human abilities are no match for things which are spiritual. God knew this, which is why He knew that we would need Jesus!

The scripture in Matthew that we discussed earlier is not a scripture for grace people like us. That's actually a scripture for those that were bound to the Mosaic covenant, an illustrated verse to remind them that they needed a Savior, because they would never be able to do that covenant on their own.

The introductory scripture in this chapter from Ephesians 3:13 (a scripture from the new covenant, the grace covenant) is one of the many scriptures that we, grace covenant folks, have to depend on! The ending of that scripture is what's most important:

## Forgive as the Lord forgave You!

This is hugely different! In this scripture, God is letting us know that He has already done the work, so my dependence is on Him to help me do it as well. My dependence on what He has already done gives me the power and ability to complete this enormous task that I can't fully complete on my own.

Learning how to depend on Christ and His finished works is a far cry from the impossible task, demand and pressure of

Matthew, where it appears that God expects me to forgive some crazy grievous act or He won't forgive me!

See, I believe that grace changes our perspective of who God is. The Mosaic law described Him as untouchable, hard core, this I'm-going-to-get-you-for-every-little-thing-you-do-wrong type of God, but grace is just that! It describes Him as loving, approachable, the I'm-here-with-you-for-everything-that-goes-wrong type God.

I thank Him for that! I thank Him for Grace! That's how Jesus is described in John 1:14:

> *And the Word was made flesh and dwelt among us, and we beheld his glory, as if the only begotten of the Father, Full of Grace and Truth. (KJV)*

Full of grace and truth—everything we needed ahead of time to live this life as a believer. We as believers in Christ have to learn that everything we are as true believers, as those who have accepted the righteousness of God by belief in Christ Jesus are totally dependent upon what Christ Jesus has done. The shedding of His blood, his death and his resurrection completely took care of everything that we were unable to. And at the top of that list is forgiveness!

Forgiveness can be one of the most difficult spiritual processes that some of us have had to encounter, but thank God that because of grace, we are not dependent on our limited human abilities to forgive others. Christ and His unlimited love allow us to be dependent on Him.

# Chapter 4
# THE PAST IS THE PAST, BURY IT!

*Pressing on toward the goal for the prize*
*of the upward call of God in Christ Jesus!*
*Philip 3:14 (ESV)*

Many times, the biggest barrier preventing us from going forward is how often we struggle with our past! We live a life constantly staying in a place that we no longer reside in. It's like you move to New York City but you still give people your address in Florida.

We have to learn to let the past be the past, especially when it no longer serves purpose in our life. We have all heard the saying, "Forget the past!" Well, I don't necessarily agree with that, because as humans with a mind and a brain, we store memories regardless of if we want to or not, so even if we try, we are not able to just erase something from our memory. Most times we think we can, but trust me, it's buried deep in your subconscious just waiting for the right moment to sneak its little head out! So, trying to forget the past may not be the best option!

Actually, we have to understand that sometimes remembering is good! Even though those memories might be painful, they can help you get to a place where you no longer allow that pain to happen to you again.

One thing that we have to do is learn how to control and decipher the thoughts of our past that try to take us back to painful places. At times, this can be a difficult task, but we are a powerful species with great ability to stop any thought from controlling our moment! We have the power to stop the Strongholds! (refer to Chapter 2). Your Heavenly Father made you that way.

Moving beyond the past can most times be difficult because as humans it is our very human nature to want justice, to seek revenge, to taste blood! We sometimes compare this narrative to sharks and how they seek after blood once they know that it is near, and even though we make this reference often, it actually isn't a very good reference to compare sharks and humans in this way! Especially if the humans are said to have a new nature and have been made righteous by the blood of Jesus.

So, yes, it is dangerous for blood to be in the water when sharks are near because the shark is making the assumption that food is near. But the shark is looking for just that, food—he's not mad or angry, or the blood isn't reminding him of the last time something bad happened to him. The blood is an indicator that as a predator this may be an opportunity to eat. Which is why when you're watching the news and you hear about a shark attack, it's just a shark bite, because sharks don't eat humans.

Well, maybe in the famous 1970's film "Jaws" but not in reality. Once a shark realizes that it has encountered human blood and not that of a fish, whale, seal, or some other type of sea creature, it moves on. Sharks don't like human blood, but yet as humans, this is the comparison that we try using as an example, because what we think is due to our hurt. We want justice, revenge, even death at times. In our unrenewed soul, we think we want the person who hurt us to hurt as much as we are hurting, even when they have suffered the ultimate, which is death.

Two of the men who violated me are both deceased, and at times I have to reel my soul in from still wanting them to burn in hell for the pain they caused me to feel. I literally have to speak out loud to myself, "Girl, they aren't even here anymore." Then I have to speak to the dark spirit trying to cause discord in the very soul that has already been made whole, the enemy. "Devil, you're a bold-faced liar! You will not steal my peace! I am restored, renewed, and healed! I am not that little girl! I am a woman of God! Get behind me!"

You have to remember that there is always a devil at work! He is always on his job. His resume is clear in John 10:10:

> *The thief comes only, to steal, kill, and destroy! (NIV)*

Don't let him take anything else from you!

The battle that you are in now is not with the person who violated you, it's not with the person who should have protected you, it's not with God, or even with the devil.

The battle that you now have to win is the one with you and your past.

I think to go forward, we do have to, at times, treat our past like it's gone forever from our life. We have to take it to the cemetery and bury it.

But once it's buried, we can't go back and dig it up. That's what so many of us do. We can go one month, two months, or even a couple years without reliving that past hurt, but then all of a sudden, a life circumstance, an unfortunate situation, or even a simple movie can trigger a moment. And if we're not careful, we go right back to being that eight-year-old in that dark room!

I've come to realize that you can't always stop the mind from going there, but you definitely have the power and ability to control it from staying there.

That's why being diligent in your thought life and using your words is important. I discovered that my words were so important and so powerful that many times the enemy tried to cut off my voice, tried to make it hard for me to speak.

But again, my dependence isn't on me; it's on Christ, so I tap right into His love, and I am freely able to speak what I need to move on from that moment.

We have to depend on God for everything, He wants us to. It's His will. The more we do, the easier it becomes, and the better our lives will be. He knows that our past can sometimes be a difficult task to move forward from, but He will not let it prevent you from the beautiful life plan that He has preordained for you even before you got here.

## Trust Him daily to lead you to your best life!

# Chapter 5
# THE STRUGGLE IS OVER!

*I can do all things through Christ*
*who strengthens me!*
*Philippians 4:13 (NKJV)*

God has trusted me with this journey. No one could walk it out better than me and this chapter's scripture reminds us that no matter how tough or dark our journey has been, with Christ we will win! We will make it to the finish line, and we will be better for it.

Recently I was studying the story of Joseph. Like many people, I thought I knew this story, but my understanding was enlightened with an even greater truth than I thought I knew.

In the story I begin to see the true sovereignty of God. Do you realize that after all that Joseph's brothers did to him, they were later able to live in Goshen? If you aren't familiar with the story of Joseph, please read it in the scriptures Genesis 37-50 in the Bible. Goshen, at that time, was one of, if not the most prominent and resourceful areas on the earth.

I'm sure if people really studied the story out, they would question how God would allow them such luxury after all that they had done. I know I did. I mean they planned to kill their own brother, and knew he was kidnapped and sold into slavery. That is a bit much. When I read how their life ended in beauty and abundance and saw that revelation for the first time, I'm pretty sure I had not fully adopted the nature of grace, which is, if I received grace, I must be a person who gives grace as well. I was still that "Christian" after blood and thought revenge would be better. Why should they have a blessed ending after all they did in their past?

So many of us miss seeing the goodness of God because our concern is on the penalty of what we feel like someone's punishment should be.

But I tell you this, after all that we have been through, all the pain we felt, all the hurt we have endured, if the tape is to be put on rewind, there is some hurt that you gave. There is some pain that you caused, and there are many mistakes you have made.

Thank God He doesn't allow man to determine our fate. Even in the worst situations, so many times we can see God's miraculous hand giving grace and mercy to those in need and to those we may feel like don't deserve it. And if we're honest, some of those undeserving cases are our own.

But that's God. His ways are so much higher than ours, and He doesn't think like us. Although we don't always understand it, His sovereignty reigns and is best for our lives.

Being a woman who was once a child who was sexually violated caused a lot of painful days in my young adult life, but I thank God that I chose to go to sleep every night and continue to keep receiving the sun every morning!

Now at the beautiful, privileged age of fifty, I understand things a little better, I see things a little differently and I love a lot harder, trusting that the God who has always been with me and is still there, helping me navigate this thing called life! You may not be there yet but just keep swimming and eventually all of the ashes will burn away, and the beauty will rise fourth!

I love you!

Ingrit

# Journal

*Let's talk about it!*

These questions are not meant to judge you. They are only meant for you to be honest with you. Being honest about how you feel and what you know or don't know is the first step to healing.

What is your Truth?
(What was your life's violation?)

_______________________________________________

_______________________________________________

_______________________________________________

_______________________________________________

_______________________________________________

_______________________________________________

_______________________________________________

_______________________________________________

_______________________________________________

_______________________________________________

_______________________________________________

_______________________________________________

Do you still struggle with forgiving? Why?
Do you forgive yourself?

Are you truly happy?
If so, why? If not, Why?

# What do you believe about God?

Do you know who you are?

I am praying for you. Send me an email at prayers4thewin@gmail.com and let me know if this book was beneficial to you.

God Bless,

Ingrit

# Appendix

Scripture quotations marked CSB have been taken from the Christian Standard Bible®, Copyright © 2017 by Holman Bible Publishers. Used by permission. Christian Standard Bible® and CSB® are federally registered trademarks of Holman Bible Publishers.

Scriptures marked ESV are taken from the The Holy Bible, English Standard Version: Copyright© 2001 by Crossway, a publishing ministry of Good News Publishers. Used by permission.

Scriptures marked KJV are taken from the King James Version, public domain.

Scriptures marked NIV are taken from the New International Version. Copyright©1973, 1978, 1984, 2011 by Biblica, Inc.™. Used by permission of Zondervan

Scriptures marked NKJV are taken from the New King James Version: Copyright© 1982 by Thomas Nelson, Inc. Used by permission. All rights reserved.

Scriptures marked NLT are taken from the Holy Bible, New Living Translation, Copyright©1996, 2004, 2007 by Tyndale House Foundation. Used by permission of Tyndale House Publishers, Inc., Carol Stream, Illinois 60188. All rights reserved. Used by permission.

# Author Bio

Ingrit M. Busbee is a minister of the grace of Jesus Christ. She has been known for her dynamic teaching and deep spiritual insight.

Over the years, she has taught at several churches, conferences, and retreats, sharing the message of Jesus Christ and His love for each and every human. Ingrit's service to others in ministry is marked by her heart for healing, restoration and equipping—especially those challenged by the pain of childhood molestation and abuse—to walk boldly in their faith in God.

Outside of ministry, Ingrit loves to travel, and treasures time with her family and close friends. Her life is fueled by faith, connection and a desire to see lives changed and transformed to what God desires for them to be. Ingrit is available for speaking engagements, book discussions and signings; and can be reached at: prayers4thewin@gmail.com.

www.ingramcontent.com/pod-product-compliance
Lightning Source LLC
Chambersburg PA
CBHW052359060726
47592CB00019B/1660